**ARRANGED BY LINDA SPEVACEK**

# CHRISTMAS! CHRISTMAS!

## FIVE-FINGER PIANO SOLOS

| 16 | Coventry Carol, The |
|---|---|
| 12 | Frosty The Snow Man |
| 10 | God Rest Ye Merry, Gentlemen |
| 8 | Hark! The Herald Angels Sing |
| 2 | Joy To The World |
| 6 | O Come, All Ye Faithful |
| 4 | Up On The Housetop |

Hal Leonard Publishing Corporation
7777 West Bluemound Road
P.O. Box 13819 Milwaukee, WI 53213

Copyright © 1989 HAL LEONARD PUBLISHING CORPORATION
International Copyright Secured   ALL RIGHTS RESERVED   Printed in U.S.A.
For all works contained herein:
Unauthorized copying, arranging, adapting, recording, or public performance is an infringement of copyright.
Infringers are liable under the law.

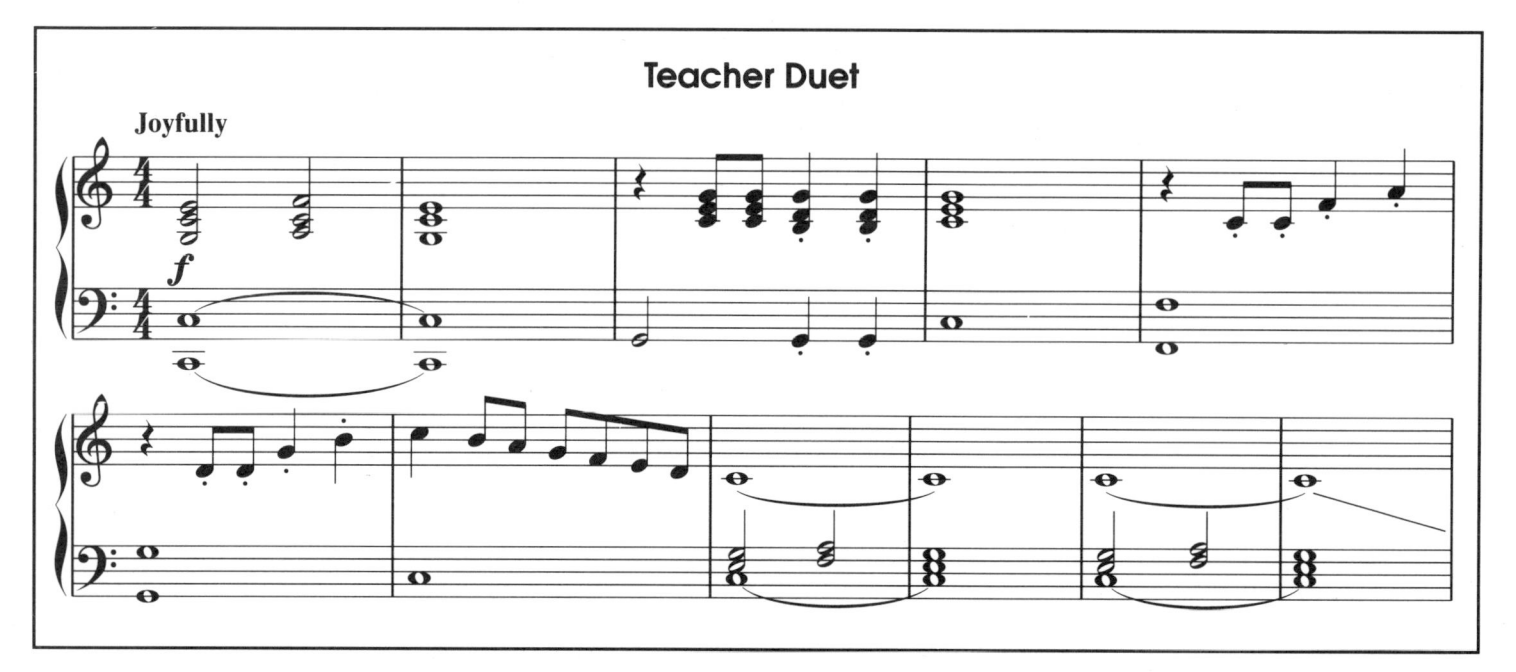

# Joy To The World

Teacher Duet

*Joyfully*

For duet, play both hands one octave higher.

*Joyfully*

Joy to the world! The Lord has come: Let earth re - ceive her King; Let ev - 'ry heart pre - pare Him room, And

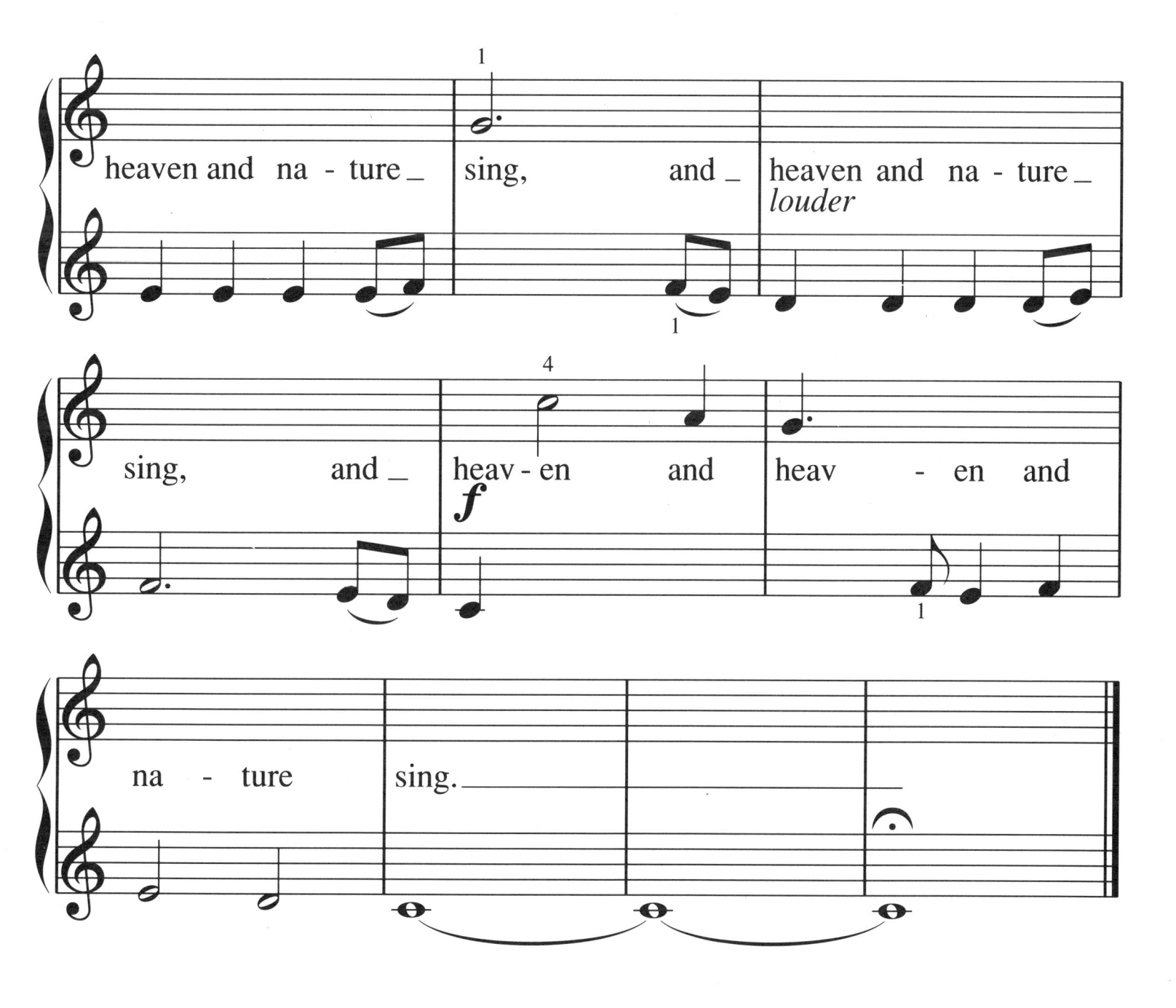

heaven and na - ture _ sing, and _ heaven and na - ture _
*louder*

sing, and _ heav - en and heav - en and
*f*

na - ture sing.

# Up On The Housetop

Teacher Duet

For duet, play both hands one octave higher.

**Brightly**

Up on the house-top rein-deer pause, out jumps good old San-ta Claus; Down thru the chim-ney with lots of toys, all for the lit-tle ones Christ-mas joys. Ho, ho, ho!

Copyright © 1989 by HAL LEONARD PUBLISHING CORPORATION
International Copyright Secured   ALL RIGHTS RESERVED   Printed in the U.S.A.

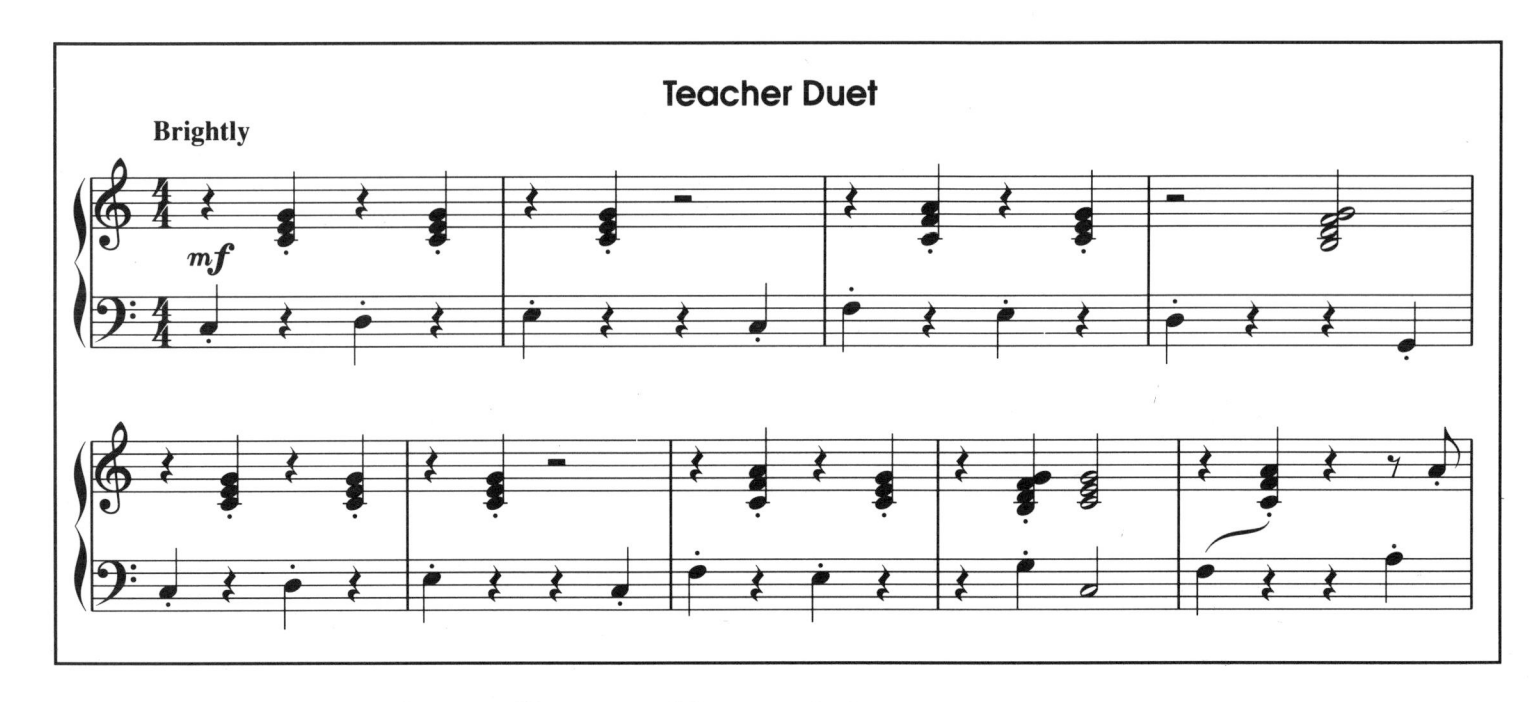

Who would-n't go! Ho, ho, ho! Who would-n't go!

Up on the house-top click, click, click, Down thru the chim-ney with good St. Nick.

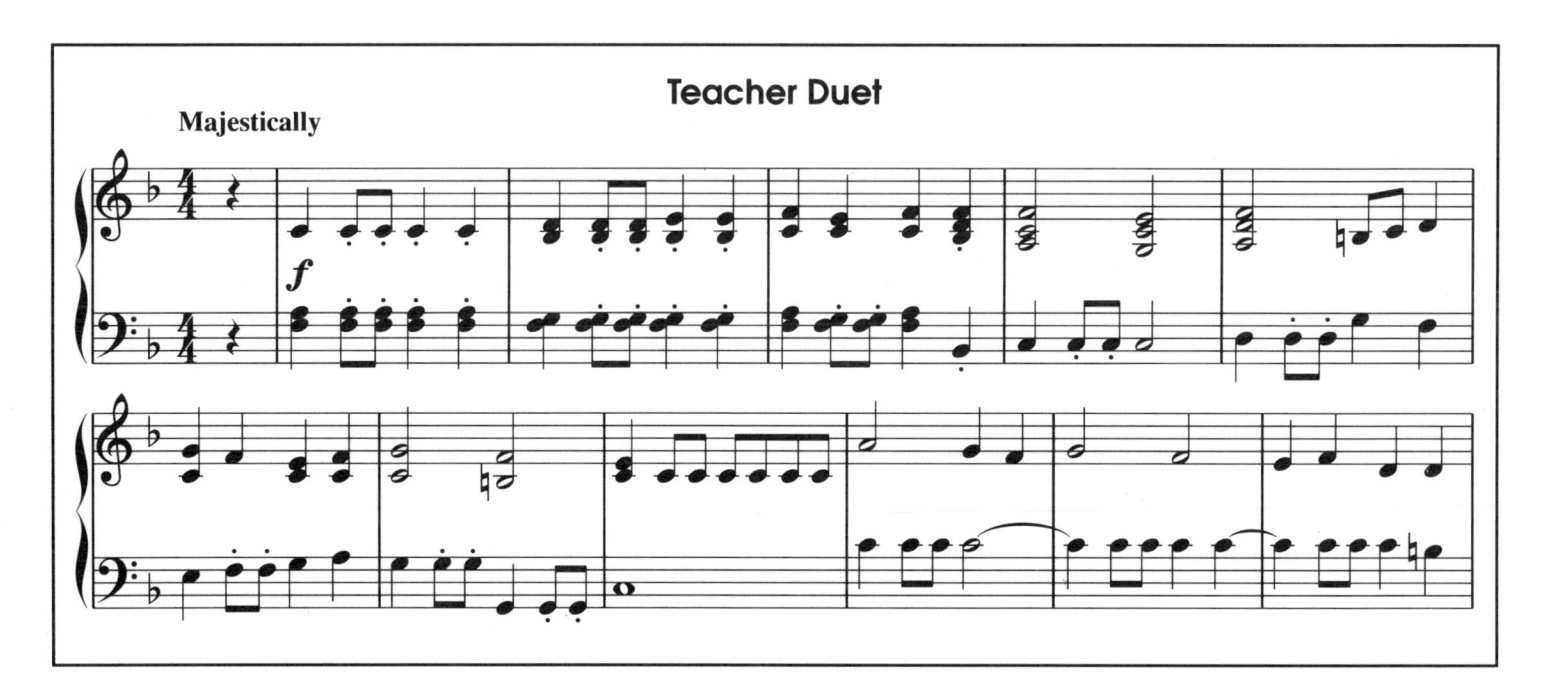

# O Come, All Ye Faithful

Teacher Duet — Majestically

For duet, play both hands one octave higher.

**Majestically**

O come, all ye faith-ful, joy-ful and tri-umph-ant, O come ye, O come ye to Beth-le-hem; Come and be-hold Him, born the King of an - gels; O come let us a - dore Him, O come let us a - dore Him, O come let us a - dore Him, Christ the Lord.

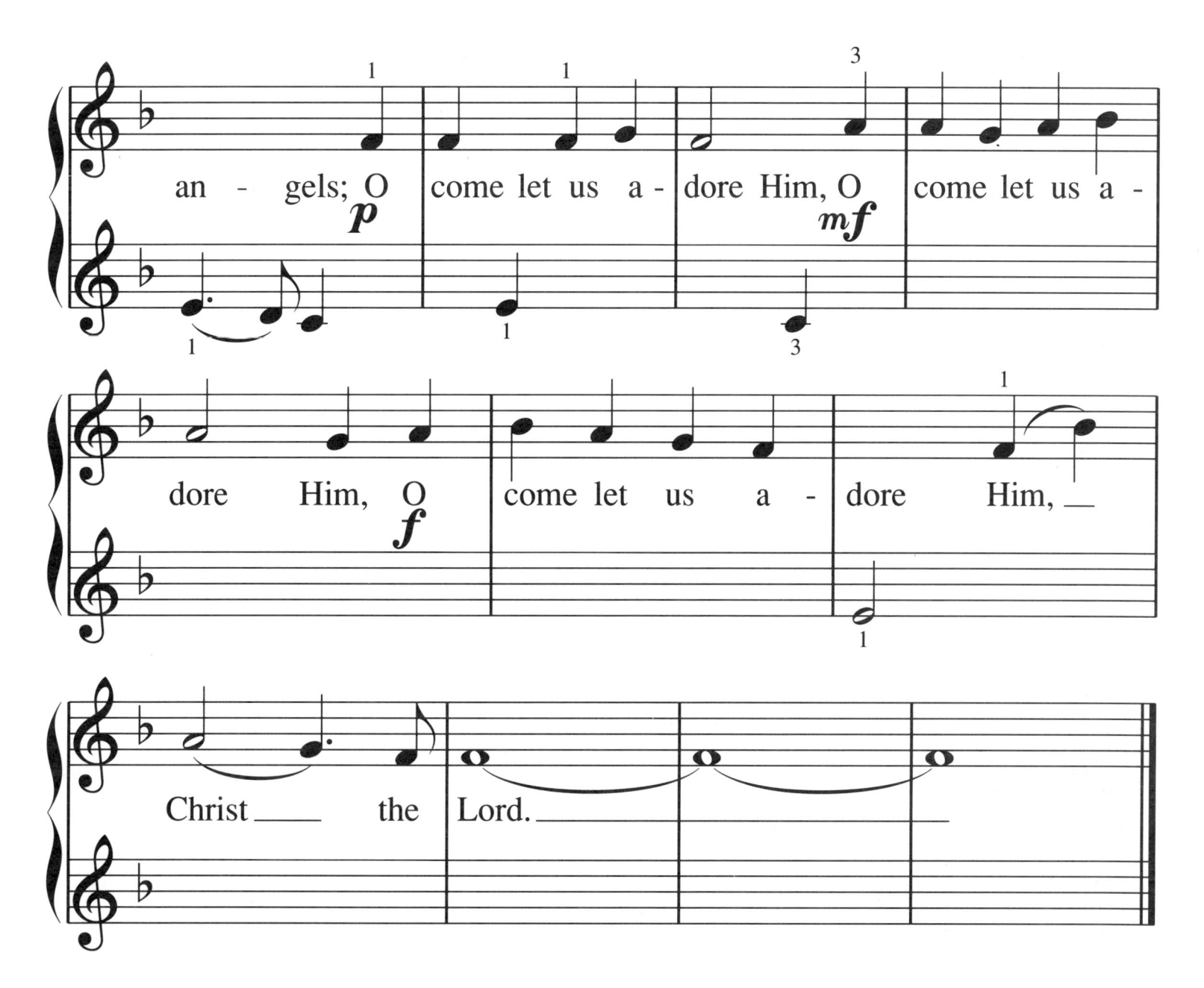

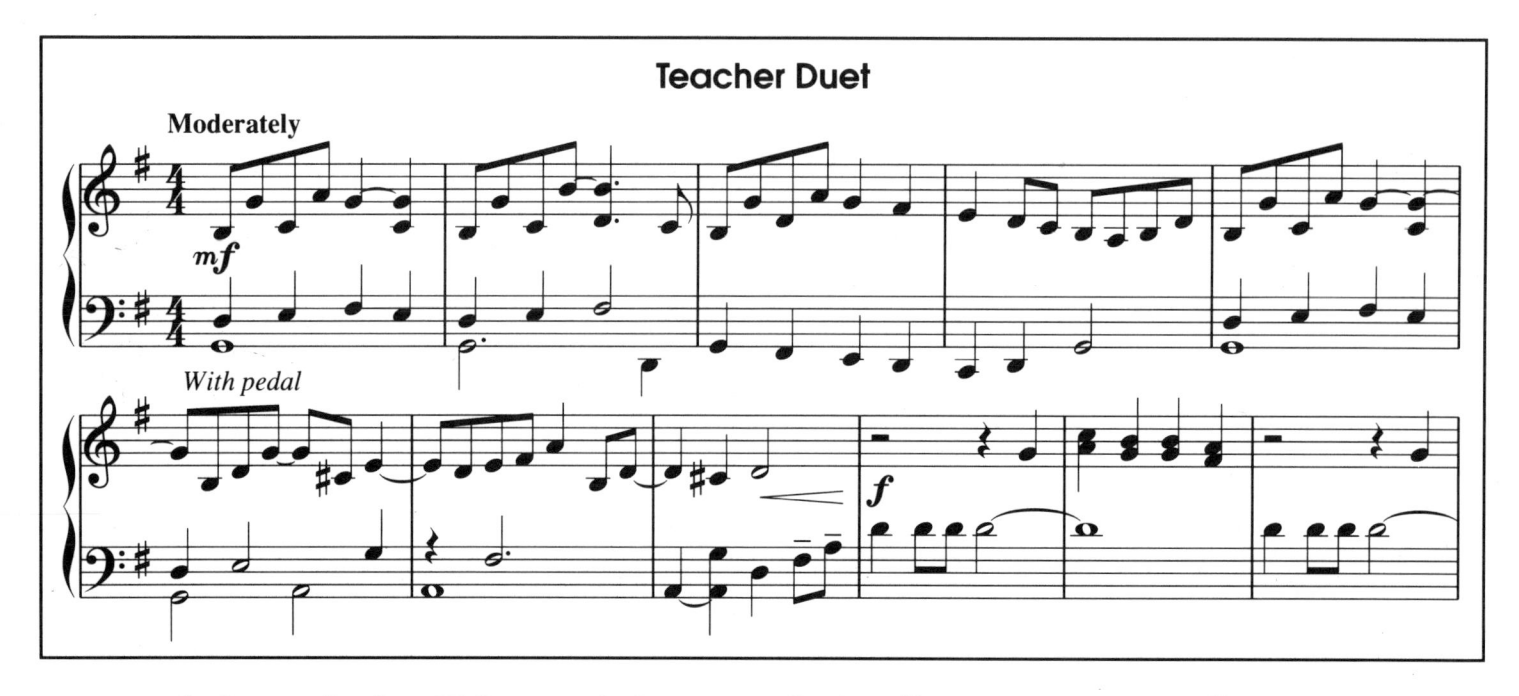

## Hark! The Herald Angels Sing

*For duet, play both hands one octave higher.*

of the skies; with th'an-gel-ic host pro-claim, "Christ is born in Beth-le-hem!" Hark! The her-ald an-gels sing, "Glo-ry to the new-born King!"

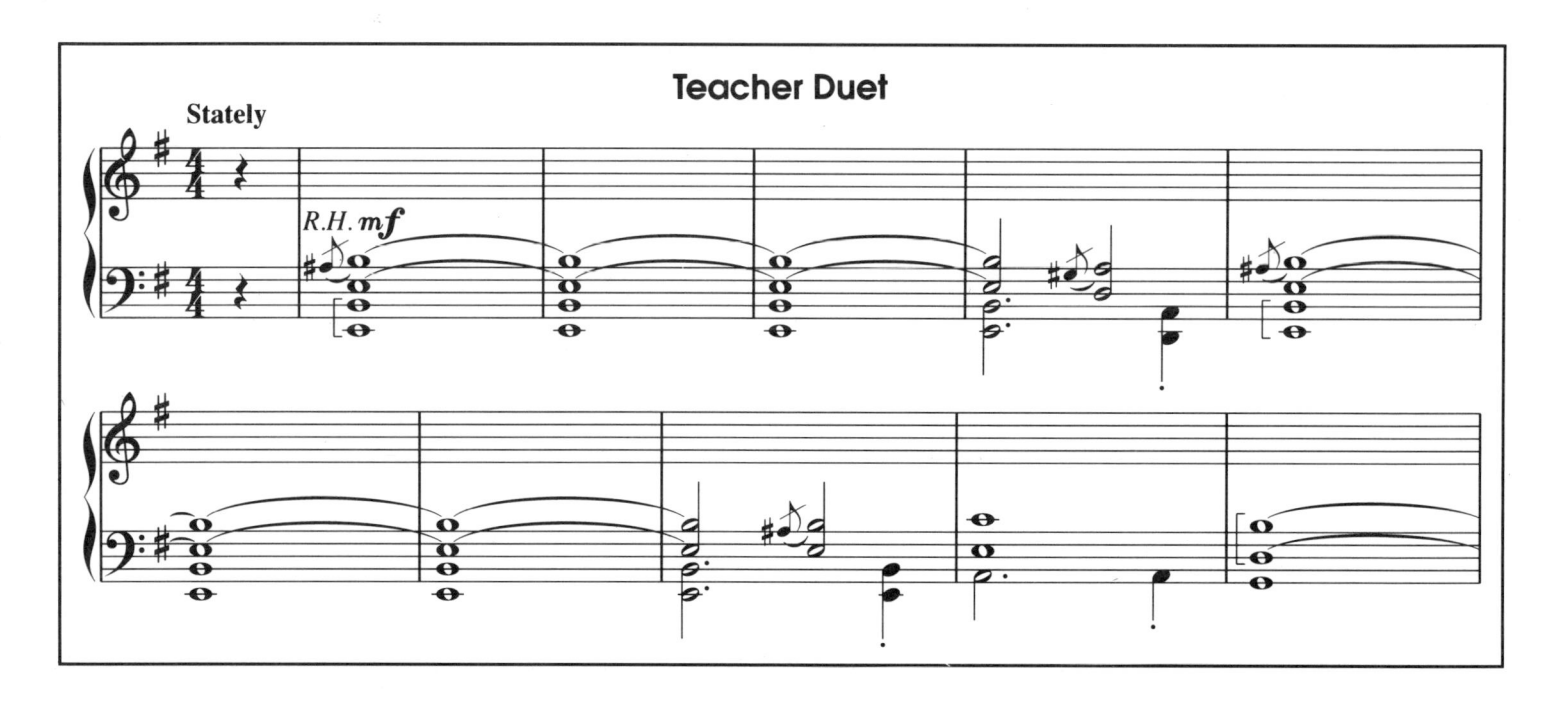

# God Rest Ye Merry, Gentlemen

For duet, play both hands one octave higher.

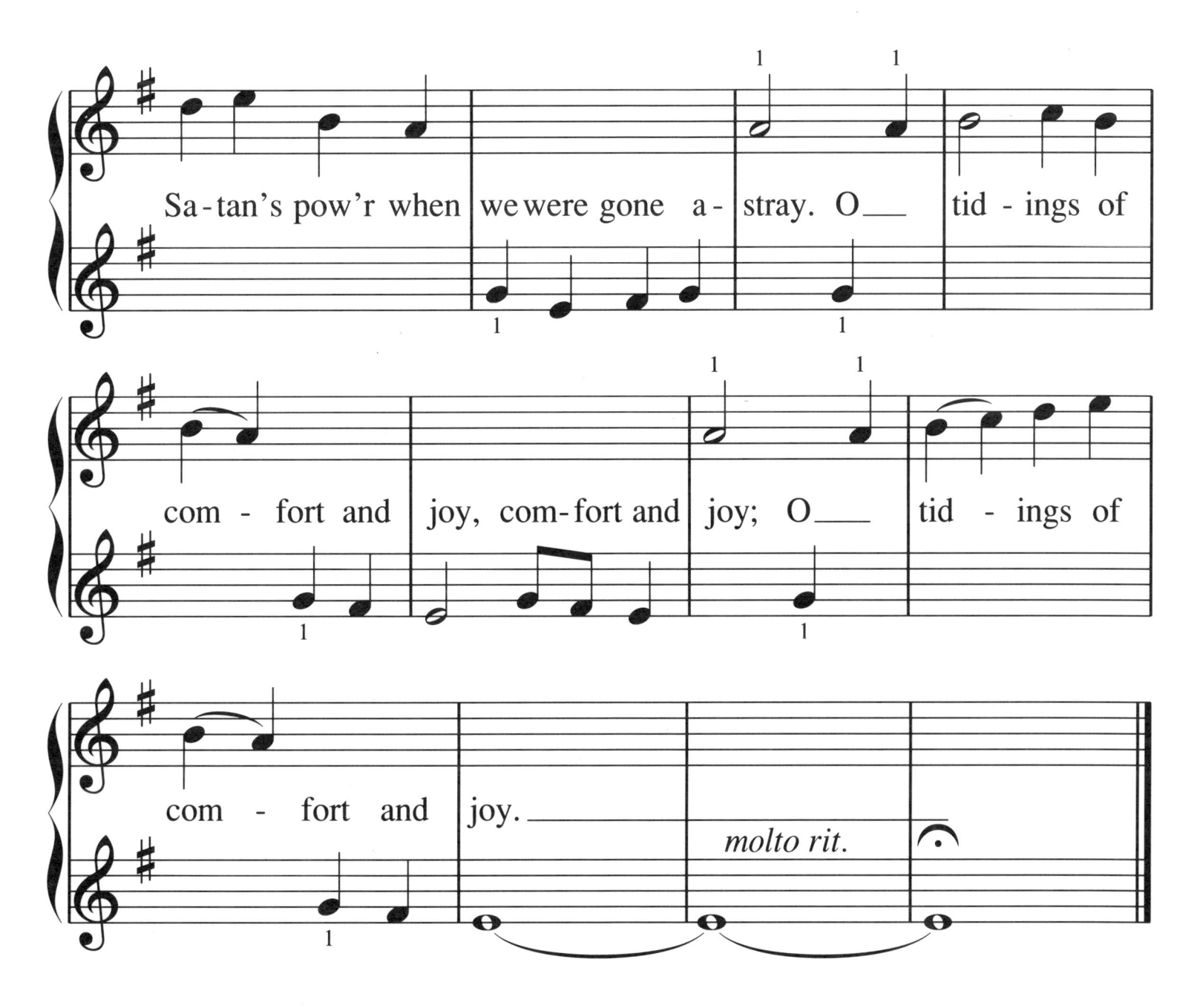

Sa-tan's pow'r when we were gone a-stray. O\_\_ tid-ings of com - fort and joy, com-fort and joy; O\_\_ tid-ings of com - fort and joy.\_\_

*molto rit.*

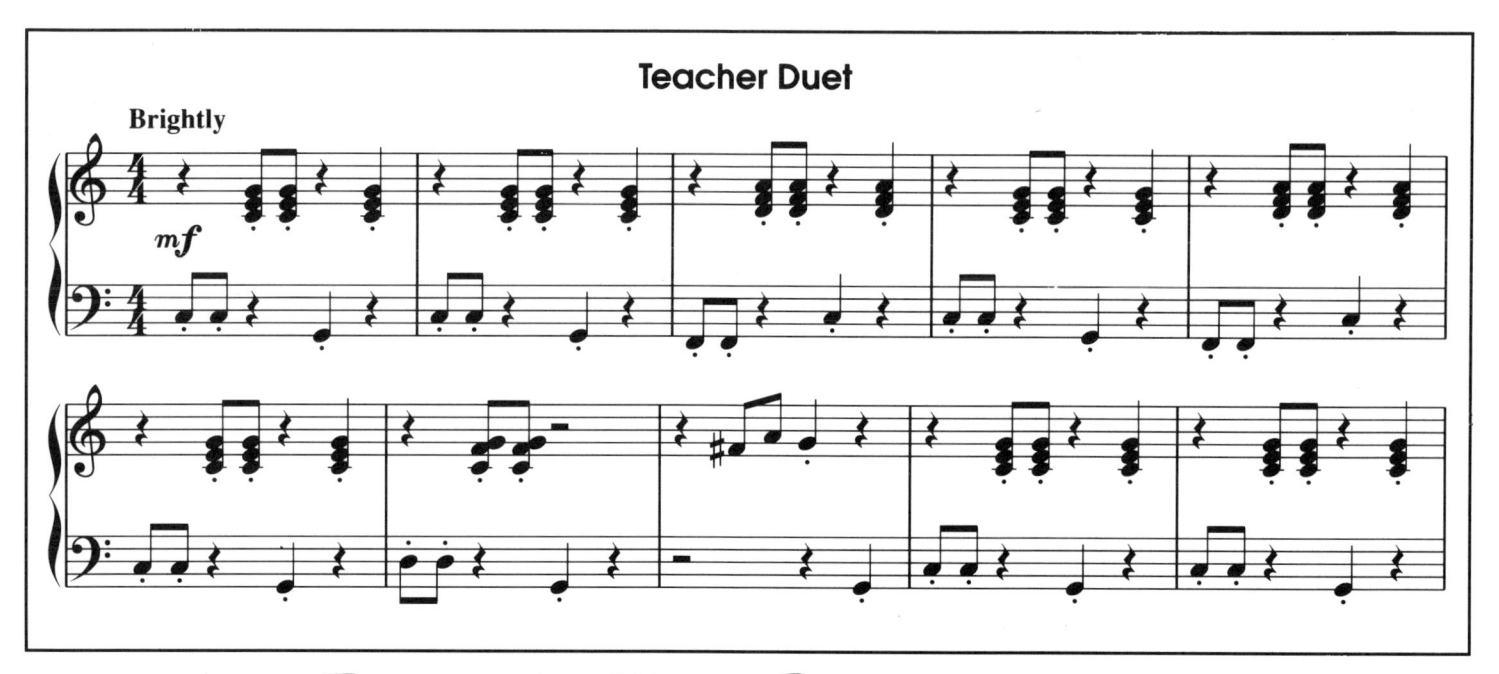

## Frosty The Snow Man

Teacher Duet

**Brightly**

*mf*

Words and Music by Steve Nelson and Jack Rollins

For duet, play both hands one octave higher.

**Brightly**

*mf*

Frost - y, the Snow - man was a jol - ly, hap - py soul, With a corn cob pipe and a but - ton nose and two eyes made out of coal.

Frost - y, the Snow - man is a fair - y tale they say, He was

Copyright © 1950 by Hill & Range Songs, Inc.
Copyright Renewed, controlled by Chappell & Co. (Intersong Music, Publisher)
This arrangement Copyright © 1989 by Hill & Range Songs, Inc.
International Copyright Secured   ALL RIGHTS RESERVED   Printed in the U.S.A.
Unauthorized copying, arranging, recording or public performance is an infringement of copyright.
Infringers are liable under the law.

made of snow but the chil-dren know how he came to life one day. There must have been some mag-ic in that old silk hat they found. For when they placed it on his head he be-gan to dance around. Oh, Frost-y, the Snow-man was a-live as he could be And the chil-dren say he could laugh and play just the same as you and me. Thump-et-y thump thump,

thump-et-y thump thump, Look at Frost-y go.

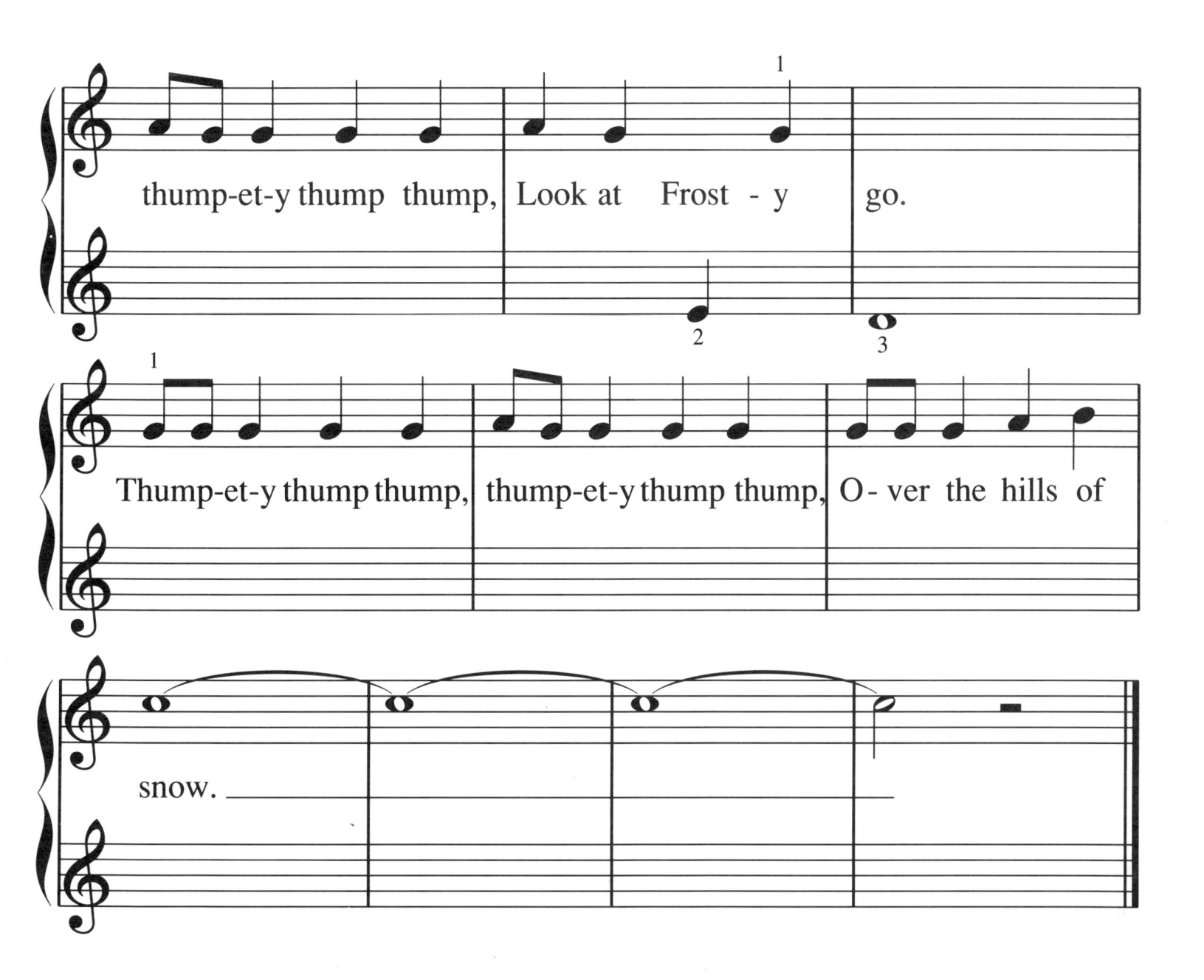

Thump-et-y thump thump, thump-et-y thump thump, O- ver the hills of

snow.

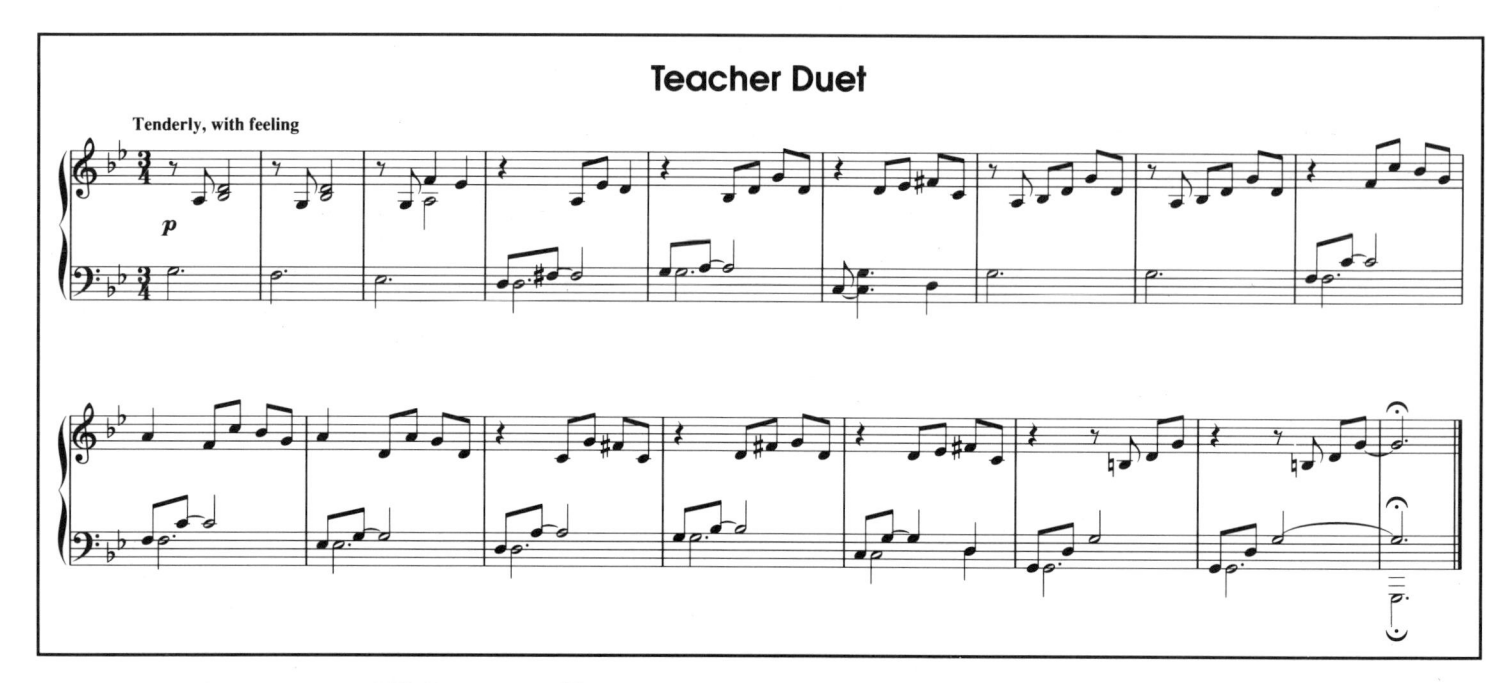

# The Coventry Carol

*For duet, play both hands one octave higher.*

**Tenderly, with feeling**

Lul-lay, Thou lit-tle ti-ny Child, By, by, lul-ly lul-lay. Lul-lay, Thou lit-tle ti-ny Child, By by, lul-ly, lul-lay.